Marseillaise My Way

Darina Al Joundi is a critically acclaimed actor and writer of Lebanese-Syrian origin. The daughter of notorious Syrian journalist, freedom fighter, political activist and exile Assim Al Joundi, Darina Al Joundi is known throughout the Arab world for her television and film roles, and has also played occasional roles in popular English-language series such as Homeland and Tyrants.

Al Joundi is also co-author with Mohamed Kacimi of a novel-length version of *The Day Nina Simone Stopped Singing* (Actes Sud 2008), translated by Marjolijn de Jager (Feminist Press, 2010), and author of *Prisonnière du levant* (Grasset 2017), a fictional biography of feminist pioneer May Ziadeh which is currently being adapted into a film.

Also by Darina Al Joundi

Novels
Le Jour où Nina Simone a cessé de chanter with Mohamed Kacimi (Actes Sud, 2008)
Prisonnière du levant (Grasset, 2017)

Plays
Le Jour où Nina Simone a cessé de chanter (L'Avant-Scène Théâtre, 2012)
Ma Marseillaise (L'Avant-Scène Théâtre, 2012)

In translation
The Day Nina Simone Stopped Singing, novel, translated by Marjolijn de Jager (Feminist Press, 2010)
The Day Nina Simone Stopped Singing, play, translated by Helen Vassallo (Naked Eye Publishing, 2022)
Prisoner of the Levant, translated by Helen Vassallo (Liverpool University Press, forthcoming)

Marseillaise My Way

a monologue
by
Darina Al Joundi

translated by *Helen Vassallo*

Naked Eye Publishing

First published in the French language as
Ma Marseillaise by Darina Al Joundi Mayenne: L'Avant-Scène Théâtre, 2012

© 2012, Éditions L'Avant-Scène Théâtre, Collection des quatre vents, 2012

© 2012, Darina Al Joundi

The right of Darina Al Joundi to be identified as the author of this work has been asserted in accordance with the Copyright, Designs & Patents Act 1988.

First published in English translation
by Naked Eye Publishing 2022

English translation © 2022, Helen Vassallo

All rights reserved

Translation of La Marseillaise with kind permission of Iain Patterson. The full text can be found on his website
https://marseillaise.org
© Iain Patterson (2012)

The quotation by Taslima Nasreen is from *Libres de le dire* (*Free to Speak*) by Taslima Nasreen and Caroline Fourest (Flammarion, 2010) and reproduced in translation here with the kind permission of the publisher.

The quotation by Djemila Benhabib is from *Ma vie à contre-Coran* (*My Life Against the Qur'an*) by Djemaila Benhabib (VLB Editions, 2009) and reproduced in translation here with the kind permission of the publisher.

Book design, typesetting and front cover by Naked Eye.

ISBN: 9781910981214

nakedeyepublishing.co.uk

CONTENTS

Marseillaise My Way..11
Postscript...57
Notes...63

Noun, the heroine of *The Day Nina Simone Stopped Singing*, has left Lebanon to make a life for herself in Paris. *Marseillaise My Way* follows Noun's adventures as she flees her home country and arrives in France. After having survived civil war, drug addiction, violent assaults, and enforced incarceration in a mental asylum, Noun embarks on a new struggle: to obtain French citizenship.

Marseillaise My Way

The scenery is made up of five lightweight screens hung with white paper, each screen measuring two metres high by one metre wide. At the start of the play, the five screens are lined up at the back of the stage, forming a white wall. The orchestral music of 'La Marseillaise' begins, and the stage is backlit, showing Noun's shadow behind the wall of screens. She belts out the anthem along with the orchestral music, rattling off the verses one after the other. She makes no effort to hit the right notes; she just wants to get the words and tune in her head. She sings off-key but she keeps going, one verse after another, until she reaches the end. She is out of breath by the time she reaches the final line: "Drive on, patriots! Liberty, cherished liberty!" The music stops.

Noun appears on stage.

Phew, I've got it...

Finally!

She is excited.

It's today, today's the day, today's my day.

My last appointment before I get French citizenship.

She stops smiling.

I've been through a lot to get here. But here I am, that's the most important thing.

She sees herself back home in Lebanon.

I spent a lot of time inside my own four walls, in my apartment in Gemmayze, in Beirut... Not far from the sea... I looked after my plants. I hid away there, waiting for the moment I could leave. I stayed in that apartment, hardly moving. I didn't see anyone, I didn't talk to anyone. I went off to film my crappy TV shows so I could earn money, pay off my debts... and leave. I wasn't allowed to go out any more, I wasn't allowed to walk or laugh or dance, I didn't even want to do any of that any more, I just wanted to leave. My city, my country, my friends, my neighbourhood, my family, everything... it was all lost to me now, I had nothing left.

When she says these words, she realises that she has lost everything from her former life. She moves forward, overcome by a calm sadness.

I smoked spliff after spliff to numb all my needs: the need to create, to work, to breathe, to walk, to love, to live.

She moves forwards again, and she is irritated.

I wanted all the nastiness to stop, I wanted people to stop looking at me as if I was a lunatic. I wanted them to stop saying...

She imitates the people she's speaking about, and the way they laughed at her.

"So, you went mad did you?"

She laughs. She becomes exactly what they were accusing her of: crazy.

Yes, I went mad.

She speaks in a threatening voice.

But watch out, because now if I kill someone I won't go…

She pauses.

I wouldn't go to prison: I'm certified insane; so I'd go back to the asylum.

She says it as if she was simply saying that she'd go back home. She pulls herself together, and remembers that asylum with bitterness.

Even the asylum was easier to bear than the people around me and the way they looked at me.

She walks around, humming 'La Marseillaise', as if to comfort herself. She walks towards the wall of white screens. It's as if she was looking right through the white paper stretched across the screens and could see herself back there. She speaks quietly to herself.

They all abandoned me.

She pauses, and then addresses the audience again.

They all abandoned me, everyone I knew. The intellectuals, the authors, the artists… the great minds!

They all turned away.

They all cheered for the man who beat me up.

She turns back to the audience, and speaks in an almost childlike voice.

See nothing, hear nothing, say nothing, that's easier, isn't it?

She moves forwards, and speaks in a more serious voice.

So I found my strength elsewhere, the strength to hold on until I could get out of there.

She stops short, and turns to face the wall. She speaks with tenacity.

I had to, I didn't have a choice. I didn't want to be exposed any longer, I couldn't be. So I hid away. (*She remembers.*) I couldn't stay in Beirut and film my shows, and I couldn't go back to the asylum in Jounieh and stare at the big crucifix on the roof.

She shies away from these memories, and turns back to the audience, speaking as if she were trying to convince herself.

I have to stay strong, I can't lose my cool now.

I'll think of all the women who have helped me to hold my head high.

I endured a war, carnage, bombs, bullets, snipers, car bombs, alcohol, drugs, men, violence, madness, myself… and now I have to endure other people!

She stares towards the back of the stage, as if she can see a ghost in the distance. She tries to look more closely, and she seems to recognise a face. She gazes intently at it, trying to see the apparition.

May? May? May?

Each time she says the name, it's as if the face was getting closer to her, until she sees it, almost on stage beside her.

May Ziadeh, is that you? You're the one who gave me strength. When I was in the asylum, you were all I thought about. In the asylum they call Asfourieh, you became my friend, my sister, my confidant. I know your story by heart. You were a pioneer in journalism, in literature, in education. You were the first girl to go to the University of Cairo, you were the star of Cairo at the turn of the twentieth century, with your literary salon that was attended by everyone who was anyone. They were all in love with you May, with the idea of you. You're the one they loved and adored, and you're the one they shut up in a mental asylum in Lebanon, you're the one they abandoned. The same woman. You fought for your rights, you fought the judges, you went to court. I wanted to fight too, like you, and make them pay for beating me up and shutting me away in a mental asylum in Lebanon, just like they did to you. I looked it up, I read all about it, I found out how you did it. I consulted experts and lawyers… I understood pretty quickly that I had no chance, because I had no rights. I'm so scared. How can I carry on living in a country where I can't defend myself? I'm not as brave as you, May. So I said to myself: go, leave, find yourself a country where you'll be safe, where no-one can hurt you ever again. May, in reading your story and learning about your life, I found all my idols, these women who have inspired me and guided me. You knew them all: Huda Sharawi, the mother of Arab feminism. Do you remember, Huda, the day of the demonstration in Cairo, when you stood up to the English occupier? That day, you pulled off the *yachmak*, that shameful square of fabric that covered your face. You burnt it in the middle of what was then Ismaïlia Square. Now it's called Tahrir Square. I'm with you, Huda:

She begins to shout out in Arabic:

Safiratt wa naftakher [Unveiled and proud!]

She walks back and forth on the stage as if she were demonstrating with all these women by chanting their slogan.

I'm with Nabawiyya Musa too: she was the first girl who stood up to the English occupier to have the right to sit for her baccalaureat. Girls weren't allowed to do it, but Nabawiyya did, she got permission, she sat it, and she did it: she got her baccalaureat. We've come a long way since then, haven't we May? But it's as if none of it happened: we've reached the end of the line, there's nowhere else to go.

Quickly, she heads behind the wall of screens, and sits down on the ground as if she were very afraid. The audience can see her shadow on the screen.

I couldn't carry on living in my country. I couldn't even carry on walking the streets of my city.

She opens one of the screens as if it were a door. Only part of her face is visible.

You know, walking along and talking to myself is my way of coping when I'm stressed, tired, or nervous. But people started to look at me strangely. So I stopped walking.

She is scared again, and goes back to the shadow behind the screens.

I was afraid of the city and its streets. I'm scared, I'm scared.

She stands up, stays behind the screens and starts gazing out. She shouts.

I need you now. Laure!

She appears and calls out.

Laure Moghaizel, you're the only one who can defend me.

She starts looking everywhere.

The only one… who will defend me.

There is a pause. She carries on searching.

Laure!

I really do need you: tell me how I can defend myself! You're the lawyer who has won the most cases. You're the one who got the vote for women in Lebanon. Not to mention inheritance rights! Before you came along, women were entitled to nothing. You fought it and you won…

She takes on an ironic tone.

But only half the battle: oh yes, non Muslim women now have the same inheritance rights as men... but not Muslim women.

And what about me, what do I do? I need you. I look around me, and all I see is emptiness.

The music of 'La Marseillaise' begins. It brings her back to the present moment. She starts to hum along with the music.

Walk, walk, just start walking again, that's all, I just want to walk without bothering anyone. But just walking, even that, was enough to wind them up.

She turns towards the screens, and takes hold of two of them as if she were opening a double door. She positions herself between them. She takes a few steps, then turns back.

I have to move away: France, Belgium? No, further away: Holland, Germany? No, further still: Finland, Sweden? No, further, even further away.

She moves forward.

Canada, Quebec! They're nice to immigrants there, they're generous, they're kind, and they even speak French: not French-French but still French. And it's a beautiful country. You can breathe there, you can eat well, and live well. Ah, I could be happy there and live in peace. So I got a visa and I went off to have a closer look around. Canada, Quebec, the people, the country, the landscapes, the hospitality, the scenery, the food, the air, everything... everything.

She steps back and bends over as if she were very cold.

But... it was so cold! Every time I wanted a cigarette I had to go outside... I froze to death every time I had a smoke! It was below zero. And I smoke a lot. No, I can't live like that. No point looking around any more. I… can't… live… in… the… cold. I packed up and went back.

She closes the two screens again. She walks behind the screens humming 'La Marseillaise', and then comes out again, and stands among the screens.

I need to find somewhere else. What about the USA? The American Dream.

She starts moving the screens around, placing some in front of others, as if she were constructing an entire city.

My friends are always telling me: what you need is New York, it's made for you, you'll feel right at home in New York, it's your city. Really? OK then. New York: Here I come!

She looks at the landscape around her. She starts walking in the streets, between the screens.

I didn't get it. You have to love concrete to love New York. And concrete is my sworn enemy. In Lebanon, everything was destroyed by concrete. Even the tiniest villages, the most far-flung, were ravaged by concrete. Concrete everywhere, as far as the eye can see. The whole of Lebanon turned concrete grey.

She is exasperated.

New York, New York, gah… I couldn't breathe in that city. And the sirens, the cars, the horns, the people, the night, the day, the dustbins, the dirt, the cracks in the pavement: it was like being back in Beirut! And then whenever I wanted to have a cigarette I had to leave the apartment building: I couldn't even smoke in my own apartment! They say that smoke travels through the pipework… So at 6am, when I wake up, I go downstairs with my cup of coffee, I go outside and sit across the street on the steps of an old building. And I meet other smokers: they call them the NFIs, the "no fixed incomes". Most of them are artists or musicians. They're not junkies or alcoholics, or thugs: there are plenty of those, of course, but they're not like that! They're just people. The city has turned its back on them. And the older ones are still working. I saw them in the streets with their high-vis jackets...

She makes traffic control movements with her arms.

Traffic control. They have to do it, otherwise they don't eat and don't have healthcare... just like back home.

She lets the audience into a secret.

You know, I'm not poor: middle income... well off, even! Well, back in Lebanon, even I couldn't afford insurance. I lived in fear. I used to pray I wouldn't fall ill. You can die at the hospital door if you don't have the magic sum: two thousand dollars in cash. Die because you can't afford medical help? Shameful. And it's just the same in New York! America... if you don't have the magic sum, you die. I refuse to live like that. I didn't come all this way for that. So I packed up my things and went back.

The music of 'La Marseillaise' begins. She sings and hums along with the music quietly, without really making much effort. She puts the screens back where they were. She is exhausted.

Back to my room, my four walls, my plants, my crappy TV shows...

She is about to slump to the floor but she pulls herself together.

No, I can't give in or give up. I can see them now, all those women I've met through my work, on my travels. I would never have thought that in standing up for them I would be standing up for myself. I thought I was better protected than them. Right from the start I decided to stand up for them, right from my first film.

She takes hold of the final screen and puts it in place to finish her wall.

It was never released, never saw the light of day, or a single cinema screen. Why? Because it was about women. Worse, it was about Arab women.

She goes stage right towards a bottle of whisky. She picks it up, drinks a mouthful, and sits on a stool at the side of the stage.

In the film, I had to travel across Arab countries, meeting women and telling their stories. It was like being punched in the gut! It put me back in my place alright. I had cast myself as a saviour, a defender, a superwoman. Well, those women were a lot stronger than me. They were their own saviours. They aren't victims. They fight. For example, let me tell you about… Fatma. We met in Menoufia, Egypt, in a little village called Tahwai. In the film, I was to portray Fatma's life story. Like all the women in the village, she had to do everything: work the earth, sell the crops, bring up the children, milk the cows, clean the house, feed, wash, clean, make love to her husband, if you can call it 'making love'. I lived alongside Fatma, and the women of her village, for three weeks. And just before I left…

She stands up, and as if it were a film set, she sets up the scene, adjusts the lighting, and puts the stool right in the middle of the room she has just created.

Fatma knocked at my door. I opened it and there she was, talking and crying at the same time. I couldn't understand anything she was saying. I could make out some words:

She speaks in a mixture of Arabic and English.

Leïla, my daughter, my husband, the village, crime, barbaric, nine years old, my mother. Come here Fatma, calm down. Tell me all about it.

Calmly, she sits on the stool in the middle of the room. She lifts her head and becomes Fatma.

"Noun, you're the only person I have left. You have to help me save Leïla, my daughter. They're going to kill her. I know what I'm talking about. It happened to me too."

With a lump in her throat, Noun continues giving voice to Fatma's words.

"They're going to circumcise her tonight. And she's only nine years old, at her age it'll kill her, I know it. Noun, I'm to blame, it's my fault, I didn't want her to be like me, I didn't want her to go through the same things I did."

She starts to cry.

"Every time my husband wanted her circumcised, I found reasons not to do it. I wanted to put it off as long as possible. But now I've run out of ideas, I have no more excuses, I have no-one but you. My husband will listen to you, you're an actress, that means something doesn't it?"

Noun stops, stands up, and goes out of the room she has created. She goes back to being herself.

How could I tell her? Being an actress is the worst thing of all. People look at me as if I were a whore. How can I tell her that the governments, the politicians, the secret services back home try to force the hand of well-known actresses to use them… as if they really were whores! If they refuse, they're dragged through the mud with court charges for prostitution or substance abuse, or sometimes even killed, chucked off a balcony. How can I tell her than in an airport in one of the Emirates, the girl who was stamping my passport at customs recognised me. She was so excited, and she cried out to her friends: "Come here girls, taalou ya bannat, come and see the gahba, the gahba is here!"

She moves forward and says clearly, precisely.

Gahba means "whore". How could I tell Fatma that I have been called a whore so often that I've finally realised: where I'm from, I should be proud to be called a whore. They should even change the definition of the word. In the dictionary, under the word "whore", they should put: "a free woman who is financially, intellectually and professionally independent." In the end I've realised that any time anyone calls me a whore, I should answer "Yes, I am, and proud!"

She looks back at the room she has created with the screens.

I didn't want to disappoint Fatma. I went to see her husband but I knew I couldn't change anything. The next day Fatma was in mourning for her daughter, Leïla. I wanted to tell her how sorry I was, to give her the strength to accept Leïla's death. There she was, in the middle of the room, dressed head to toe in black, standing with the women of the village. She wanted Leïla to be the last girl to die… by circumcision. She refused my condolences.

She goes back into the room and sits on the stool, speaking as Fatma again.

"The men always say that you cannot accept condolences for a martyr. My daughter Leïla is a martyr of circumcision. I will accept your condolences the day that girls like Leïla no longer suffer this fate."

Noun pauses, and then goes back to being herself.

What can you say, what can you answer, what can you do when you're faced with such bravery, when you're faced with such a woman? Nothing. I left in tears, and I felt fragile, oh so very fragile...

She starts to unmake the room and put the screens back in their places like a wall.

I made a promise: I would carry on fighting for her, carry on telling her story. Fatma, I'm here for you. I promise you. I made so many promises while I was shooting that film.

She walks forward.

And then there was... Rajia. She told me her story so that I could portray it on camera. On the first day of filming, I had to be...

She puts her hands around her neck, and pretends to strangle herself.

Aagh... Aagh... I couldn't even talk. How did she cope? She really went through that, for real. Buried. In the ground. The ground of her family farm, in Arabia. Buried up to her neck. The men of the family were standing in a circle around her, stones in their hands, ready to slaughter her. It was the day of her stoning. There she was, left for dead. It was the gardener's wife who saved her.

And what was Rajia's crime?

She lets go of her neck and walks forward.

Who cares? Nobody has the right to do that. She fled, she never went back to her country, she never saw her daughter again.

She turns round, goes towards the stool, and picks it up. She sets it beside the wall of screens and sits on it. She pauses, and then returns to the leitmotiv of her apartment in Beirut.

Back in my four walls, in the apartment in Beirut, in Gemmayzeh, not far from the sea… I need them, I tell myself their stories over and over, I see their faces again. They give me the strength to keep going, to fight, to leave…

Leave, leave, leave…

She stands up, hears the music of 'La Marseillaise', and starts to hum along.

France! I know the country, I speak the language, even if Lebanese-French isn't really anything like French-French. France! I've already worked there, I've already lived there, it's the most secular country there is, the country where people… where I will be safe.

She speaks with all the enthusiasm she can muster:

France, HERE I COME!

She starts singing 'La Marseillaise'.

"What do this horde of slaves,
Traitors and conspiratorial kings want?
For whom have they wrought their vile iron chains?
Frenchmen, this outrage is prepared for us!
What can we do to stop them in their plan
To return us to the slavery of an evil past?"

She looks at the audience.

Dear God!

She doubles over.

Noun, now's not the time to argue about the words. Right now you need to get all your papers in order.

She walks towards the wall of screens.

You know what? I've fought all my life to get my papers. Let me explain:

She starts making corridors with the screens.

My father was Syrian, and since he opposed the first Assad regime, he had to flee Syria, and his papers were revoked. My mother is Lebanese. I was born in Lebanon. But in Lebanon, nationality is not passed down by the mother. Of course not, because she's a woman, and so you can't give her the same rights that men have. That would mean admitting that she's a citizen in her own right. I've spent my life running around trying to get residency permits… in my own country!

In 1995, I was finally allowed to apply for Lebanese citizenship. But after all I'd been through, being slandered, beaten up, locked up… the papers seemed meaningless: once you're mad, you're always mad in the eyes of the law. In France, I'm going to do everything right: no risks, no mistakes, nothing that could jeopardise my right to belong. Finally I'll feel safe. A country where I'll feel equal to everyone else regardless of colour, background or gender. A country where I can express myself freely without paying a price for it.

The music of 'La Marseillaise' strikes up. She tries to remember the words as she walks up and down the corridors, between the screens. She barely hits a right note, singing off-key all the time. She isn't really trying to sing well, she's just trying to remember the words. Sometimes she tries to hit the right note but she doesn't manage it.

"What! These foreign cohorts
Would have themselves ruling our courts!
Sending their mercenary phalanxes
To murder our warrior sons…"

She seems to have forgotten the next line. Then she remembers it, and carries on singing, faster than before:

"They would bring us, chained, to our knees
As they rule over us."

She is concentrating so hard on the words that she sings off-key.

"The vile despots would be…"

She stands in front of the final screen, and cries out the rest of the song:

"… Masters of our destiny!
Tremble, tyrants and traitors
Who bring dishonour to good men
Tremble, for your evil schemes
Will…"

She is still concentrating on getting the words right. She makes a mistake, stops, and tries again.

"Tremble, for your evil schemes
Will get their come-uppance!"

She is pleased to have remembered the words, and starts singing faster.

"We are all France's soldiers in the fight against you
Ready to man the breach…"

She pauses, trying to remember the final line.

"…should our young heroes fall."

She is happy to have remembered it, and starts to run behind the screens, shouting:

"Tremble, tremble, tremble, tremble…"

She stops at the final screen, exhausted.

As soon as I get to France I'll follow my plan, get my papers, then ta-da! I'll have my passport. It's been like an assault course to get to this point: the last day before my naturalisation.

She pauses. She starts to think about the word she has just uttered.

Naturalisation: why choose that word, naturalisation? What does 'naturalisation' even mean?

She moves forward towards the audience, and tells them knowledgeably:

"The introduction of plants or animals to places where they flourish but are not indigenous".

She smiles.

So I have to bloom here like a plant to be naturalised? Naturalisation, naturalised. Why not choose: obtain nationality, become French? Anyway, it's a big day and I'm going to do what I like to do best: I'm going to walk. Sometimes I feel as though I left my country just to have the right to walk around. Walk, walk, walk all the way to my appointment. Noun, look around you, look at where you are, look at the morning, the first rays of sunlight that make everything seem brighter. Come on then, let's go to this appointment, walk on!

The music of 'La Marseillaise' strikes up again. Noun starts to walk, going back and forth. She sings to herself; she is happy to be setting out on the walk to her appointment, she runs and starts humming loudly to the music of 'La Marseillaise'. Then she breaks into song.

"Citizens, take up arms
Form your battalions
March, march,
Spill the enemy's blood

Over the land!"

She is happy with her rendition of 'La Marseillaise'. A feeling of joy has crept in on her, and keeps her going as she walks towards her appointment. She talks while walking.

It's strange all the images that keep coming back to me, it's as if I can see my whole life passing before me as I walk. Nobody believed I'd really do it: leave everything behind and come here. Everyone who called me crazy carried on saying it, and kept jeering at me: the crazy lady will become a tramp, we'll find her under a bridge, freezing to death. Well, no, the gamble paid off, I won! It hasn't been easy to get here. At first, when I turned up and applied for a residence permit…

Out of breath, she appears at the end of the wall of screens, and starts to explain.

On top of everything else I wanted to work as an actress, it's the only thing I know how to do, telling stories…

She uses the corridors and screens as offices.

So I needed a permit that's very hard to get: the creative category for artists and entertainers. Otherwise, every time I wanted to take on a job, I'd have to get permission from the Employment Ministry and, every time, I'd have to go through the same process: the long waits, the health checks, the visits to the town hall… the list goes on. To get that permit, you need a contract for at least nine months: I don't know many actors who get such long contracts.

She speaks proudly.

I did, though, thanks to my theatre work. Before the premieres, I went back and forth so many times to get my work visa. After I got my first one, every nine months I had to go through the same process again, and every time I was sick to my stomach, fearing the worst.

She comes forward, and steps out from the corridors of offices, speaking in an aside.

I come from a place where the simple fact of going into a government building can cost you your life. Don't even get me started on town halls and police stations.

She goes back to the corridors of offices.

And then every time I had an appointment I had to get there super early, wait outside until the doors opened, then queue up and go in, get frisked, take off my shoes, jacket, and why not all the rest of my clothes while we're at it, as if I was going on a flight. Once I got into the waiting room, I had to hand over my file at the reception desk. You take a ticket with a number on it, and wait until your number flashes up on the screen that tells you which desk to go to. It's true that I was treated better there than in the town halls in Lebanon. But that sick feeling never went away.

She comes out of the corridor.

Every time I go to the town hall, I say my goodbyes to the city, to my apartment, to my husband... it's strange how your body remembers things. The day we went to see the flat we wanted to rent...

She forms the apartment with her screens.

...I had a quick look round.

"OK, let's take it!"

I didn't make my decision based on the view, the floorspace, the location or the rent, oh no! I made my decision for a completely different reason.

"Why is this the one you want?" he asked me.

"Look at the bathroom, it's perfect. A bomb could never get to it. And bullets wouldn't stand a chance."

Neither my husband nor the estate agent with us understood what I was talking about, although it's very simple. You should always look for the safest place in an apartment.

She explains as if she were reciting an instruction video.

In the event of a bombing, you have to be able to take shelter. The place of shelter must have several protective walls that cannot be broken down. As I was explaining it to them… when I saw the looks on their faces… I realised what I was saying.

She falls silent for a while.

It's a good thing I left.

She forces herself to smile in order to hide her emotion.

It was time.

She hums her 'Marseillaise' again, and starts putting the wall of screens back together.

Since I got here, I haven't stopped working. With my work I travel a lot. Every time I have to travel, it's a nightmare to get a visa. I don't want to have to wait in embassies any more, or put up with people staring, or the way the employees are treated. And let's not get started on what happens at airports! For every trip I take, I prepare a set of jokes to keep the officer who has to stamp my passport amused. Whereas Karine (we travel together a lot for work), never even has her passport.

She imitates Karine.

"I don't need it", she says.

Shocked, her hand over her mouth, she moves forward and says in a single breath.

Eeeek! How can you not have your passport, your ID card, your car registration document, your birth certificate and all the papers you can possibly imagine whenever you go anywhere, even in your own city?

She seems annoyed.

And if there's a checkpoint, what do I do, huh?

She realises what she's just said.

Stop it, you have to stop thinking like this!

I just want to be treated like everyone else, or at least like Karine… Even if she is blonde. Maybe I should just dye my hair blonde, that's more Western, right?

I need to find a solution that makes me feel like I'm a human being.

She thinks about it.

The ten year visa! So I don't have to deal with these temporary visas any more and I can finally put together an application for naturalisation.

She plays with the word "naturalisation" as she says it.

Once again, the waiting, the queues, the numbers, the wasted days, the documents to provide, each more ludicrous than the last, and the constant risk of not getting my papers.

She stops.

They've already turned me down twice. Want to know why?

She imitates the clerk.

"Madam, in your first two years here, you didn't earn enough money."

She is distraught.

I thought I was going to die, I thought they were turning me down point blank for any kind of permit. I saw myself back there, just before I left, sick to the stomach, terrified of everyone, terrified of upsetting them, having to defend myself constantly against intimidation and violence. I saw those streets where I couldn't walk freely any more, and I wept, I wept, I wept on the clerk. Poor man, he didn't know what to do with himself.

"Calm down, Madam, you can still have the nine-month visa, just not the ten-year one."

I stopped crying.

The second attempt was not exactly covered in glory either. On the day of my appointment, there were a lot of clerks off work. The ones who were there were trying to persuade people to come back another day. Everyone was afraid. We all wanted to stay and wait. I don't know why, but when it came to my turn the man said: "Madam, if you agree to come back another day, I'll give you a priority pass."

She says it as if it were the keys to the kingdom.

I looked him straight in the eyes, and gathered up all my courage.

"Yes, yes, OK, I'll come back another day."

He was so relieved and grateful, so I pushed him a bit.

"Wait a minute! I agreed to change my appointment because

you really needed someone to help you out, so you should stand up and thank me on behalf of the French Republic."

She laughs.

He stood up.

She imitates him.

"Madam, on behalf of the French Republic, I thank you for having agreed…"

She bursts out laughing, and then stops.

The whole palaver was pointless: they turned down my application again.

She waits a while.

There was only one thing left to do:

She stresses each syllable of the word as she says it.

Na-tu-ra-li-sa-tion.

I have the five years of residence you need to be eligible, so I can put in an application.

She speaks in Arabic and then in English.

Tarik al jouljoula. And so the ordeal began.

Exhausted, she forms a quarter circle with the five screens, like the stage of a theatre.

To put together the elusive application, every visit to the town hall is a half-day wasted. And you should see how applicants get treated: the things they put you through so you can find out which application form you need to fill out, and how to fill it in. The whole thing's a charade, performed right before your eyes. You get there, you take your number, and you wait. Of course there are families there too, so there are kids who are crying and fidgeting because they've been waiting for two hours already. And it's right at that moment that the lady in charge will come and have a go at the parents. The numbers flash up one after another. Each number corresponds to a person, and with all the different accents the dialogue can get surreal.

She acts out the scene.

"How old is your child?"

Noun puts on an Asian accent.

"Yes, yes, I arrived in 1999."

The clerk speaks as if the applicant were deaf.

"No, I asked you for your child's age!"

"Yes, yes, we live in the 13th arrondissement."

And so it goes on! And of course there's no privacy. You don't get asked all these questions in a separate office, it all happens in front of everyone else. Once, someone started giggling for no reason, and we all ended up laughing hysterically.

We were all glancing at each other, all afraid of getting told off by the lady in charge, which in the end is exactly what happened. I only had one thing on my mind: making sure that the whole room didn't get to know everything about my life and my secrets. My number flashed up, I went to sit in front of the lady. After every answer I gave, she shouted: "What?"

And so I said it again, louder, so that she could hear. And along with her, the whole room got to hear.

She acts out the scene with the clerk.

"Have you ever been married?"

She answers quietly.

"Yes, I've been divorced three times and married four times."

"What?"

Noun repeats her answer at the top of her voice.

"I've been divorced three times and married four times."

She gave me a strange look.

"Oh! Well then you need to bring all the official marriage certificates, and you need to bring all the original copies of the decree absolutes…"

Noun speaks directly to the audience.

How could I tell her that I didn't get married and divorced so many times just because I felt like it? It's not because I like collecting marriages and divorces or that I'm trying to be like those celebrities who are always getting married and divorced…

How could I tell her that where I come from, you can't live with a man unless you're married to him, that when I had had enough of being married and wanted to live as I pleased, I went through hell. At any time, if a neighbour felt offended by my way of life (which could influence the girls in his own family), that neighbour could call the police to restore order to his neighbourhood and protect his offspring.

I always keep a plastic bag with my stuff in it right by the door, just in case… If a neighbour calls the police, I'll take my bag and I'll get the hell out of there… So I don't get dragged down to the police station and branded a whore.

She stops, stunned.

That word, again and again, "whore": how is this happening? We should set up the club of "proud whores". I'm sure there are others like me. I even met one in France: Taslima Nasreen. She's a writer from Bangladesh. She wrote a book… and went through hell.

She remembers that book, and what Taslima went through. Fear takes hold of her. She wants to run away from that fear, she starts to run behind the screens.

Five hundred thousand men in the streets, with machetes, knives, ropes and guns, all shouting, screaming, calling her a whore and demanding that she be hanged.

She shouts.

Tell them, Taslima!

She falls silent, then turns towards the audience, stops, and goes to stand in the middle of the stage. She speaks as Taslima.

"In the history of the world, as soon as a woman rises up against the patriarchy, talks about emancipation, and tries to free herself from her chains, she gets called a whore. I firmly believe that if a woman wants her freedom, wants to be an equal human being, she should be worthy of this label. It's a title that should be considered an honour. Of all the accolades I have been given, I consider that one to be the greatest recognition of what I have achieved in my life."

After a long silence she moves forward, and becomes Noun again.

How do you tell that neighbour, the one who wants to call the police, and how do you explain to this woman, the one shouting at everyone, that I got married so many times so people would stop calling me a whore.

OK, I'm not going to bang on about it now, I have other fish to fry, I have other papers to provide.

She rebuilds her wall of screens.

I have to list all the addresses in all the cities I've lived in since I was born, list all the schools I attended, provide certified copies of my parents' identity papers. Copies of official birth certificates, copies of official identity cards, copies of any criminal records, list of all the jobs I've ever had in my life. And so it goes on… Fortunately, I have the memory of an elephant and I remember all the details.

I'm tired.

She sits down on the floor.

Since I got here, with everything I've seen, everything I've lived through, everything I've gone through, I swear that if I didn't need these papers so desperately I wouldn't have stuck with it for so long.

The music of 'La Marseillaise' begins. Towards the end, She recites a verse of 'La Marseillaise', not having the energy to sing it.

"Frenchmen, as magnanimous warriors
Bear or hold back your blows
Spare these sad victims
That they regret taking up arms against us
But not these bloody despots
These accomplices of Bouillé!"

She asks a question of no-one in particular:

So who's this Bouillé?

Not getting a response, she goes back to her 'Marseillaise'.

"All these tigers who pitilessly…"

She tries to remember the last line.

"Ripped out their mothers' wombs!"

She pauses, and looks at the audience.

Then after the lists and the documents there are still the exams, the tests I have to sit, and the evidence I have to provide of my involvement in social, cultural and intellectual life. That one was easy: I sent them the press folder of my first show…

She's proud of herself now.

Four hundred pages! Thanks to that tour, I know France-France better than a lot of the French-French…

Oh, I almost forgot: the most important part, the bit that will finally allow me to fulfil my wildest dream.

She stands up, and opens her arms out wide.

The song!

She looks at the audience.

Oh yes, you have to learn 'La Marseillaise' by heart, words and tune.

She chuckles.

That's what my nationality is depending on? Can you imagine it, me, right there in the middle of the city hall?

She faces the audience, puts her hand on her breast, and sings:

"Arise patriotic citizens
The day of glory is at hand!"

There's a reason why I've been singing this whole time: I'm afraid I'll forget the words and all my chances of naturalisation will vanish. I can't let that happen…

"The bloody banner of tyranny
Has been raised against us…"

She carries on singing the tune, and hits a wrong note.

Damn.

She speaks to herself.

I have to concentrate, I have to find the right words to convince the man that I'm "selective immigration".

She waits a moment. Then she turns around, as if she were in a perfume advert.

Yes, that's me.

The music of 'La Marseillaise' strikes up, and she walks to the back of the stage, behind the screens.

I thought I was moving to the most secular country in the world. It's true that it's still a lot more secular than a lot of other countries, even if its secularism is under threat. I thought that here, women were more fortunate, had more of a chance to fight, not to make bad choices, not to be influenced by men who only want to control them. I thought that culture and education would give them a better future, the means to free themselves. But everywhere I go I see women wearing veils and burkas, girls who have chosen to wear them.

Why?

Back home, the answer is simple: lack of education, lack of choice, lack of schooling, lack of knowledge, lack of awareness, lack of possibilities. They are pressured, forced, intimidated into wearing them. So why do I see these veils everywhere over here? What would these girls say to their sisters back there who refuse to wear the veil and get beaten up for it?

She pokes her face out between two screens, and looks at the audience.

Like Souad, a 35-year-old woman from Sudan.

She comes out from between the screens, moves forward towards the audience, and speaks.

She's walking in the street with her husband. She's wearing a veil, of course. At one point, the veil slips down, and Souad tries to put it back. Just at that moment, an officer of the morality police starts shouting at her, and threatens to beat her with his truncheon if she doesn't put her veil back on. Her husband turns on her too. And she says: "No, I don't want to put this veil back on".

I don't know where she found the strength to stand up for herself. Blows rained down on her: the policeman, the husband, passers by in the street. She ended up in the police station handcuffed, whipped, slandered, repudiated. Women in Sudan get a whipping just for wearing trousers.

She is enraged.

What would the girls over here say to Souad?

She pauses.

Did you know that in France-France the law that forbids women from wearing trousers… has never been abolished? They don't teach you that at school, do they? Women of France, if you're wearing trousers, you're breaking the law…

How has it come to this?

Back home the answer is more obvious. Decades of totalitarian regimes that keep the population in ignorance and poverty to keep them under control. And after all those years and all they did, there were the Arab revolutions.

She walks towards the back of the stage, chanting in Arabic: "the people want the regime to fall". Breathless, she stops and sits down on the ground between two screens.

With all those revolutions, back where I'm from, things have changed. There is hope, they're going to build something new, maybe one day I might be able to go back... No, no, no. After a revolution, a country needs a long time to rebuild itself. And I don't have time, not any more. After everything they'd done, the only person they had left to turn to was God. And so now it's the Islamists who occupy all the positions of power. Not for long! It just needs time... it needs time... No, not for long, I'm sure of it. Just the time it takes to show their true colours, the time it takes for people to realise that cosying up to Allah doesn't make them better or more honest. It just needs time, it needs time... But I'm counting on them: Hala, Fadia, Aïsha, Jalila, Fatma, Mouna, Souheir, Samar, Razan, Givara, May, Fadwa... especially Fadwa. Oh Fadwa, I'm so afraid for you! Let me take your place.

I'll shave my head like you did, I'll go off to the city of Homs like you did, I'll shout like you do, I'll look after people like you do, I'll sing with the old ladies like you do, I'll raise a glass of arak to the revolution like you do. And if they attack me, like they did you, I'll say, like you, "You will not lock me up. I am not Muslim, or Christian, or Druze, or Alawite, I am just a Syrian woman, a woman like any other. I love like any other, I have a husband like any other, I dance, I sing, and I drink arak like any other. I am free like any other." One day we will all be free.

She hides behind the final screen.

But I can't wait, I don't have time on my side any more, I have to build a life elsewhere... here. I can only try to help them... from here.

I don't have their strength: I can't stay there and fight there. I've already paid the price for that.

The music of 'La Marseillaise' strikes up. She slips the screens sideways against one another, until they are all one in front of the other, while singing 'La Marseillaise'. She tries to remember one of the verses of 'La Marseillaise'. The music comes to an end, and she starts having a go at that verse.

"We shall follow our elders into the pit..."

She starts off fast, then slows down, changing tempo again and again. She can't remember the words. She stops, and starts again.

"We shall follow our elders into the pit
Where we shall find their ashes and their epitaphs"

Now she tries to get both the words and the tune together. As usual, she is singing a little off-key, and a little off-tempo. It's starting to bother her. She stops, and starts again. She tries to remember the words, and she sings:

"We prefer to join them in death
Or to avenge them, rather than live in shame"

She gets to the end and then breathes out.

Phew!

She is at the end of the screens. She turns towards the audience, and remembers what she was just talking about.

I get here and what do I see? Everyone withdraws into their own little corner, their neighbourhood, their community. They even tried to put me in a box, but I've never let anyone do that. Let me explain.

She takes a screen and moves forward, then she uses it as if she were a teacher with a whiteboard.

Being Arab does not mean being Muslim.

She turns back and speaks to the audience.

There are Jewish Arabs, Christian Arabs, practising Muslim Arabs, others who are non-practising Muslims, there are even secular Muslims, atheist Muslims and Muslims who are only Muslim on paper. And yes, they are unbelievers. Eeeeek… how shameful! But you're fed a whole load of rubbish. And you take it at face value. You shouldn't believe everything you're told. You shouldn't just accept everything blindly. I'll tell you how it was in my family, and maybe that will reassure you.

She places the screen in front of her. The audience sees her shadow on the screen as she imitates her grandfather.

My mother's father used to do his daily prayers. Work is the most important thing of all. You must never stop work to do your prayers. Islam makes it easy for you: Addine yossr wala ossr. You can make up your daytime prayers in the evening, when you get home. It's called Al Kadaa. It's the same for Ramadan: you should never stop work to fast, otherwise God doesn't count either your prayers or your fasting.

She pokes her head out from behind the screen.

Oh really? God has nothing better to do?

"You must never walk in front of me while I'm praying".

She peeks around the screen again.

It was my favourite game. Every time he started his prayers, I would walk in front of him. To pray in peace, he had to do it behind locked doors.

She stands up, and moves the screen aside.

One day I made a suggestion to the sheikh at the mosque opposite where I lived in Beirut: instead of waking me up every day at 4.30 in the morning to call Muslims to morning prayer, why not set up an arrangement with the mobile operators like the ones you have here, O2, Orange, Vodafone: free wake-up call for morning prayer! I think that over here, with crappy jokes like that, they'd name me Racist of the Year.

She takes the screen and puts it back with the others.

So, coming here, seeing what I see and hearing what I hear, and realising that it's just accepted without question, it makes me sick! I even saw a good Muslim who had made a folding screen for his prayers with a little bonus feature: the inside of the screen was covered with wallpaper exactly like the kind you see in mosques.

She tries to ululate, but can't quite manage it.

Gah… oh, if only I could ululate. There you go, another discovery: an Arab woman who can't ululate, yes, there is such a thing.

There is a silence, and then the music of 'La Marseillaise' strikes up, and she walks in front of the wall of screens as if she were thinking to herself. The music stops.

I'd really like to know who told all the girls over here that they had to wear the veil! And let's not even get started on the burqa! OK, Noun, stop dishing out your opinion, no-one cares what you think.

She thinks some more, and as she walks she says in a low voice:

OK, OK…

Then, as if she has found the answer:

OK. Look at the teachings of sheikh Mohammed Abdou. He was the Mufti of Cairo, you know, the Mufti of Al-Azhar, the highest authority in Islam. I've read his complete works: five thousand pages. In 1900, he made laws, fatwas: about halal meat, the veil, divorce, or rather divorce by repudiation, polygamy, co-habitation, prayers, and work.

He said the same thing as my grandfather: work is as important is prayer, you should never stop working to pray... even the Mufti himself said it. He wrote about everything, and I promise you that what he said is completely different from the Islam that I see here. So why not try to make his ideas known? And what about the teachings of Nasr Hamed Abou Zeid and all those great men who fought to offer a different understanding of Islam, so that it could evolve...

She walks as she thinks, and turns back towards the audience.

Why should we let the others have everything their way?

She has a sudden idea.

I'll do it too, I'll get on a soapbox in the neighbourhoods they call "disadvantaged", I'll stand in the middle of the street and hand out books by Abdou, Kacem and Abou Zeid to passers by.

She goes towards the screens and speaks to them as if they had become Abdou.

Abdou! Drag them out of the Middle Ages! Abdou, who's going to set them free? Ya Abdou, come here, we need you.

She addresses the audience.

We need a new Abdou.

She moves forward.

Why not give Kacem Amin's *The Emancipation of Women* to these girls who want to wear the veil or the burqa and be the second, third or fourth wife? I don't understand anything any more.

Where I come from, people fight against these shackles, they fight to free themselves from the chains. And here...

She cries out in rage.

...the world has gone mad.

The music of 'La Marseillaise' begins, she tries to regain her composure, then starts singing 'La Marseillaise' in a low voice, as accurately as possible. With the last verse, emotion gets the better of her.

"Drive on patriots
Support our avenging arms
Join the struggle of those who defend
Liberty, cherished liberty
Let victory come to our banner..."

She falls silent. She turns towards the audience.

Imagine a woman like me who turns up... or any other woman who comes over here from back there. A woman like me who also fled to escape injustice, oppression, violence. A woman like me whose father gave her the strength to fight for her country, for all these women humiliated by the Family Code.

She sees a woman's face before her.

In your eyes I can see...

She smiles.

...my eyes. I see the Bedouin woman, the gypsy woman, going from one country to another, from one continent to another, searching for the place where... Free. Djemila Benhabib, far from your Algerian homeland, you speak for me too,

Silence. She speaks as Djemila.

"Above all, never try to label me, brand me, or nail me to a community. Others have tried and failed. My community is all of humanity. My religion is the Enlightenment. Montaigne is mine just as much as Averroès. Never try to tell me that Spinoza, Nietzsche, Gramsci and Voltaire don't belong to me. They belong to me just as much as Averroès, Khayam, Abou Nawas and Ibn Arabi."

Noun addresses the audience again.

There you go, that says it all.

So then, imagine that all those women arrived here and ended up being trapped by the laws of their home country… condemned to starting the same fight all over again.

She walks quickly while looking at the audience. She grabs the stool, and puts it in the middle of the stage. Calmly and deliberately, she continues.

Many women end up divorced by repudiation in their home country: their husband only has to say the magic words: talek talek talek, three times, and then get it recognised by exequatur in France. And the woman is cut off, stripped of her rights. And it gets worse: now husbands can repudiate their wives by text message or WhatsApp. You have to move with the times, right?

I even heard that they were trying to pass a law which would allow people to be governed by the laws of their home country.

She can hardly believe what she's heard.

What? Why?

I fled from such practices. I decided to come and live here.

I hope it will never happen.

I want to be treated like the women here.

She regains her composure.

One evening I was watching TV... I like doing that. I saw a report about a French-French woman who was brave enough to try and bring a court case against her husband, who was very violent. And she won. The journalists and the humanitarian associations all held her up as a hero.

Did you know that over here a woman dies as a result of domestic abuse... every other day. I was so happy for this woman... but I couldn't help thinking of another woman, a 26-year-old living in Germany. She didn't have the right to the same legal justice. And why? Because she was of Moroccan origin.

She speaks calmly.

We are all equal in the eyes of the law, aren't we? There is no race, colour, religion or gender, right? When I found out about the details of the story, it sent shivers down my spine. Frankfurt, January 2007.

She speaks without showing any emotion.

A female judge dismissed this woman's request to initiate divorce proceedings on the grounds of domestic violence. And why did she dismiss it? Because the couple was originally from a Muslim country. And apparently, according to the Qur'an, a man may beat his wife.

So the victim ought to have expected that kind of treatment. The judge even said that the husband's honour had been violated.

She is shocked.

Fortunately, the whole thing turned into a major scandal. The judge was taken off the case.

She is outraged.

What does all this mean?

That the men who beat me up over there could come here, beat me up and lock me away again? And this woman, this judge, would let them get away with it!

She feels very alone, and speaks under her breath.

I'm scared.

She gets up silently, takes her stool to put it back in its place, stops and looks at the audience. She seems terrified.

In England it's even worse. They say that it's unavoidable, inevitable, that certain aspects of sharia law will make their way into British society and law, and even the former head of the Church of England, archbishop Rowan Williams, said it would happen.

She pauses.

Why change the laws? Do you think that in changing them you're respecting my culture and the culture of all women? No, poetry is part of my culture.

She walks a little way and then sets her stool down.

Abou Nawas, Al-Mutanabbi, Al-Hallaj, wine, they're all part of my culture, the Arabic language is part of my culture, music and dancing are part of my culture.

She looks at the audience, and addresses them directly.

Not much more than a hundred years ago, Christian women

covered their heads with scarves, didn't they? And no-one says to you today: Christian women, wear a headscarf! Nobody says to you: the headscarf is part of your culture! So why do they say it to us?

She places the stool on the ground with all her might and heads off behind the screens. With each of the following statements, she tears through a screen.

I dream of a day when… no woman will wear a veil, a wig, a burqa, or anything that hides her. Not because the law says she shouldn't or society says she shouldn't, but because she doesn't want to. I dream of a day when… all women will have access to education, to culture, and to a job. I dream of a day when… no more women will die at the hands of husbands, fathers, or brothers. I dream of a day when… there will be no more double standards. I dream of a day when… all men will want gender equality.

She steps through the first torn screen.

I dream of a day when… all women will be proud to be women.

A long silence. She comes back to the moment, and walks towards the audience.

Do you know what they want me to do now?

A test… When I found out about it, I went online immediately, I sat it, and I passed.

She addresses the audience as if she were making them sit the test, singling out people in the audience with her finger.

Why was the Eiffel Tower built?
    a   For the Universal Exhibition in 1889
    b   As a tourist attraction

    c   To set up television aerials

What is the national anthem of France?
- a 'The Marseillaise'
- b 'The Versaillaise'
- c 'The Pimpolaise'

Who was Brigitte Bardot?
- a A film star
- b The founder of a fashion house
- c The first female boxing champion

What is Michel Platini known for having played?
- a The violin
- b Football
- c Chess

Who was Edith Piaf?
- a A singer
- b A cycling champion
- c An ornithologist

Who were the first people known to have settled in France?
- a The Cretans
- b The Gauls
- c The Francs

The music of 'La Marseillaise' strikes up, and she draws back.

The Francs, the Francs, the Francs...

then she speaks angrily.

This test is an insult to my intelligence!

Suddenly, she turns on herself.

Noun, shut up and sit it. You need it to be able to vote. Isn't that what you want?

Yes, yes, I want to be able to vote.

She walks forward.

I'm going to let you into a secret: I've never voted. I wanted to but…

With her hands she makes a gesture of desperation.

Wasn't allowed!

My friend Omar used to say: "My greatest wish is that I'll get to vote before I die". And he died… before.

She stops thinking about Omar, it's as if she had said for herself "I hope that I'll vote one day before I die". Then, turning to the audience, she starts to address some of them directly.

Have you voted? And you, have you voted? And you, do you want to vote? Do you vote?

The music of 'La Marseillaise' plays softly, while Noun says in a pretentious voice.

"No, I don't want to, I've never voted, I don't like voting, I'll never vote".

She turns her back to the audience, and shouts:

What! There are entire nations who dream only of that: being allowed to vote. I dream of being able to exercise that duty, that right as a citizen of the French Republic, and vote. You'll see, when I get my citizenship, I won't miss a single election: from the presidential election right down to the resident's association in my apartment block. And do you know what I'll do for my first act as a rebellious citizen? Gather a million signatures in support of making the blank vote count.

She falls silent. She realises that she's half-way through gathering a million signatures to make the blank vote count but she hasn't yet got her citizenship, she still has to provide the final documents. She starts taking the torn screens one after another and assembles them to create a cage.

Papers, papers, papers... endless papers. Every day they ask me for a new document, a new paper... to certify. I can't cope with all these papers any more. One of these days I'll turn into a certified document. I can't cope any more. I'm tired of papers. I have no more papers left to present, that's it, nothing more.

She has finished building her cage and she goes into it, and doubles over on herself.

I'm scared. I'm so scared.

They'll give me a document to sign too. How can I sign it? What would I say to my father?

She stands up, and speaks to her father as if he were in front of her.

"Dad, we fought. Syria is free. I got my passport back. Look. How can I tell you that I renounced..."

She turns on herself savagely.

They can't ask me to do that. They can't ask me to renounce my origins.

She goes to the door of the cage and speaks to the audience.

No, it can't be true, it's just a rumour, put about to scare us.

She turns on herself, and shouts at herself.

Shut up Noun, you have to do it.

She speaks to herself fiercely.

Yes, yes, I have to do it, I will do it. I must do it. I need those papers, I need that passport. I'll renounce my origins.

She opens the screen, and then speaks as if to an inspector.

Sir…

She is speaking so quietly she can barely be heard.

…I renounce my origins.

She speaks quietly to herself.

No, it can't be true. It's not possible. They can't do that.

She turns on herself angrily.

Noun, stop talking. Noun, stop thinking. Noun, stop stirring. Otherwise you'll end up in the street, beaten up and locked away like you were back there.

She stops short, turns towards the audience and looks straight at them.

I didn't come all this way just to censor myself, and if that's what France is, then I won't get on very well… or maybe I will.

She comes out of the cage, and she walks forwards, looking straight in front of her as if she were looking at the inspector. She speaks decisively.

Sir, I've filled in all the papers, I've signed all my documents and had them certified. I pay my taxes, I know France-France like the back of my hand, I've never been in trouble with the law, I speak French-French. I am 'selective immigration'. I know 'La Marseillaise' by heart, words and tune, I even know who Bouillé is. But now I ask you to sign a paper for me and guarantee that the French Republic will remain a republic: free, fair, equal and secular.

She stops, and turns on herself.

Who do you take yourself for? You'll get a kick up the butt… and you'll be sent on your way!

She answers herself.

Huh!

Then she moves towards the audience, and speaks calmly.

They turned down my application for citizenship…

Madam, your professional integration is incomplete.

In her head she says: it's a prank, it's a joke. Then she bursts out laughing. She walks straight on, and leaves the stage singing. She is overcome with emotion while singing; for the first time she masters the words and she sings the Marseillaise her way.

"Citizens take up arms
Form your battalions
March, march,
Spill the enemy's blood
Over the land."

The orchestral music of 'La Marseillaise' rises in crescendo as the lights slowly go down on the cage of torn screens.

Postscript

By Darina Al Joundi

I'VE ALWAYS SAID THAT ART CAN CHANGE LIVES, and now it's changed mine, though I'd never have believed it. In writing *Marseillaise My Way*, I wanted, first and foremost, to pay homage to all the women fighting for freedom, a community of women amongst whom I count myself. When I toured France with my first show, the audience always said to me: "You're so brave!" And I always wanted to reply: "You think I'm brave? What would you have said if I'd told the stories of the women who have inspired me instead?"

That was the starting point for this latest adventure. All through the tour with the first show, and while I was thinking about and writing *Marseillaise My Way*, I was chasing after my papers, and I said that once more life was giving me a well of inspiration.

A few days before the début of the play in Avignon in 2012, and just before I left for the theatre festival, I got a card telling me there was a recorded delivery letter waiting for me. I went racing off to the post office. A letter from the Interior Ministry was waiting for me there, but I didn't dare open it straight away.

I left the post office, went down the street a little way, and then I stopped, opened the letter, and started reading. The words and letters went fuzzy, and tears started to stream down my face. My citizenship application had been turned down.

Straight away I called Danielle, my friend and agent, to tell her the bad news; I called my friend Marjorie, who was distraught at the other end of the line, and then Caroline and Fiameta, my friends and support network, thinking perhaps they could help me, but I could barely speak, I was just sobbing down the phone.

I got to Avignon. While I was rehearsing the show at the Théâtre des Halles with my director Alain Timar, I had to add in the turning down of the citizenship application at the end of the show.

And that should have been the end of it. The festival opened, and just like in 2007 with the first show, I was on stage at 11am. And just like in 2007, by the third day the theatre was full and carried on that way until the end of the festival. The public came to see me, and people in the industry, and most importantly of all, as it turned out, the press. Everyone was horrified by the ending and by the real-life outcome.

On the 21st of July, an article about my show, 'Take up arms, citizens, though I am not one of you' appeared in *Le Monde*.[1]

The next day, I got up as usual at 6am, got myself ready and set out on foot through the little alleyways in Avignon that I love so much. I stopped by to have a coffee in my friend Fred's bar, and then off I went to the Théâtre des Halles.

I took the first turn on the left, it's the same route I've taken since the start of 2007 when I came for the first lot of rehearsals. It calms me to walk through those streets, sometimes I bump into Alain on his bike on the way to the theatre; we both have our little routines, our little obsessions, and we're always laughing about it. I've always felt that the moments I spend with Alain at the Théâtre des Halles are very special, each of us at our own desk, in our own corner with our own bits and pieces, spending hours and hours working, developing our work and pushing it further. Alain always finds, in his direction and his staging, just the right idea to give a theatrical tone to my words, and his actor's eye, his questions and his perspective help me to step back from the words and immerse myself deeper into the show. Meeting Alain at the Théâtre des Halles has been my good luck charm. Alain and Laurette Timar have been, right from the start, a support which still gives me

---

[1] 'Nathaniel Herzberg, 'Aux armes, citoyens dont je ne suis pas!', *Le Monde*, 20 July 2012.

strength, they have welcomed me and opened the doors of their theatre and their home to me.

I've written a lot while wandering through the streets of Avignon, I like to look at the names of the streets and memorise them, I particularly like the rue d'Artaud just before you turn right into the rue du Roi-René which takes me to the performers' entrance, I rang the bell, and it was Laurette, who also runs the theatre, who opened the door.

As always, Alain was already there, getting the canvas ready for his other show, where he makes art live on stage.

He was with Sohee, his intern.

As soon as I got into the room, Alain said to me "Hey, guess what? They called you here at the theatre to give you your citizenship".

He was all smiles. I didn't believe him. I stared at him.

I was cross and I said to him: "Alain, please, don't joke about that. You know how exhausted I am with all the hoops I have to jump through".

He said "I'm not joking, go up with Laurette and see for yourself, you really did get a call from the Ministry of the Interior yesterday afternoon, here at the theatre. They even left you a message."

I shouted "What?!"

Then, I don't know how, but I raced up the stairs to Laurette's office four at a time. She was with Nathalie, the PR manager.

As soon as I got to the door, Nathalie looked at me and said "The Ministry of the Interior called you yesterday and left you this message."

I said "So it's true, it's not a joke!"

Nathalie said "Listen to the message yourself".

She played the message: "This is a message from the Ministry of the Interior on behalf of Mr … for Darina… We saw the article in *Le Monde*. Please could you contact us directly on … so that we can process your application."

I couldn't believe my ears, my eyes, my life. I ran back and forth in the office without knowing what to do with myself, I opened my mouth to speak and a cry of relief came out, and laughter and tears. I couldn't keep my emotion in, I couldn't get any words out, only laughter and tears. Laurette and Nathalie were as overwhelmed as me, they had tears in their eyes and they were smiling.

I can honestly say that the play that day took on a new meaning for me, a different tone.

When I got back to Paris, I presented my appeal. Every time I got a phone call, with every new ray of hope they sent me, I got ever more overwhelmed, I couldn't quite bring myself to believe in it. I was afraid it would all come to nothing again. Even when the Ministry official called me in person to tell me that I would get my citizenship, that the response to my appeal had been positive, I couldn't quite believe it, and I said to my friends:

"We can't celebrate it yet, it's not official yet."

On the 10th of October 2012, my name was written in the official Journal of the French Republic.

I became officially French.

I had a copy of the journal in my hand. I walked along the banks of the Seine with tears in my eyes. But this time they were tears of joy, of relief. I called all the friends who had helped me so that I could thank them. Everyone was shouting with joy at the other end of the phone.

And everyone asked me: "So will you change the ending of *Marseillaise My Way*?"

No, because in the play, Noun didn't get her citizenship. Not yet anyway.

Once again, life was showing me Noun's journey.

Right around the time I became French, in the midst of all the euphoria, I went to Belgium to shoot a short film with Bavi, a wonderful young woman of Kurdish Iraqi origin. It's a film she was putting together for her Masters.

The main character, who I played, is a Kurdish Iraqi seeking political asylum in Belgium, and that meant that we went to do some filming in a refugee centre.

Right at the moment when I was over the moon, when I was jumping for joy because I'd got French citizenship, I found myself face to face with this centre and its occupants.

I'll be honest: it was a five-star hotel compared to the refugee camps that I've seen back home, but that doesn't make the suffering of the refugees in these European centres any less real.

I saw them, of all nationalities from countries torn apart by conflict: Pakistan, Afghanistan, Eastern Europe, Kurds, Iraqis, all of them. And more recently Syrians too, these men and women who feel imprisoned, humiliated, and who are clinging to the only thing they have left: their dignity.

They try with all their might to keep smiling, like one amazing young Syrian man, Dany, who was always making jokes and playing the fool to try and raise a smile from the poor souls in that centre.

I said to myself: How can I dare to talk about the difficulties I've had to get my citizenship when they're going through all of this! I had the tenacity, the good fortune, not to go through the same route as them, not to have to come seeking political asylum.

At no point did I feel any anger towards the countries that were hosting them. Quite the contrary.

But I was furious with our countries, that turn these young people, these nations, into refugees, these people who had the misfortune to be born on the wrong side of the world, where dictators think nothing of slaughtering an entire nation just to stay in power.

Noun didn't have to pass through these refugee centres, but, like many others, her struggles were no less painful, oppressive, surreal and humiliating.

But my dear Noun is a fighter who will keep on fighting and who always ends up winning.

And so I, Darina, say a big thank you to the audiences who have supported me, to the press, who made the officials take action, to the Ministry of the Interior, to the Minister, and to all the friends who have worked hard so that my French citizenship became a reality and not a fiction.

Thank you to life.

D.A.J.

N.B. I was finally able to vote for the first time in my life, in France, at the age of 45. Thank you.

Notes
References to figures from Arab culture and literature

May Ziadeh (p.14): May Ziadeh (1886-1941) was a Lebanese-Palestinian writer who grew up in Egypt and held a literary salon there. After a series of personal losses she returned to Lebanon, where her family imprisoned her in a mental asylum. Her life is the subject of Darina Al Joundi's second novel, *Prisonnière du levant* (*Prisoner of the Levant*, Grasset 2017).

Huda Sharawi (p.15): Huda Sharawi (1879-1947) was an Egyptian nationalist and pioneer of Egyptian feminism. She was the founder of the Egyptian Feminist Union.

Nabawiyya Musa (p.15): Nabawiyya Musa (1886-1951) was one of the founding figures of twentieth-century feminism in Egypt. She was a writer and educator who campaigned for girls to receive equal education and independence.

Laure Moghaizel (p.16): Laure Moghaizel (1929-1997) was a Lebanese lawyer and a tireless advocate of women's rights.

Fadwa (p.41): Fadwa Soliman (1970-2017) was a Syrian actress who was prominent in the 2011 uprising against Bashar Al-Assad. She died in exile in Paris.

Abou Zeid (p.45): Nasr Hamed Abou Zeid (1943-2010) was Professor of Arab Literature at the University of Cairo, and held a doctorate in Islamic Studies. In 1995, after he wrote his thesis, he was accused of apostasy. He was forced into exile, and only returned to Cairo two weeks before his death. He is buried there.

Kacem Amin (p.45): Kacem Amin (1863-1908) wrote *The Emancipation of Women* and *The New Woman*, and was nicknamed 'the father of female emancipation' in the Arab world. He was one of the founders of the Egyptian nationalist movement for independence as well as one of the founding members of the University of Cairo.

Djemila Benhabib (p.47): Djemila Benhabib is a journalist and essayist. In 2012 she received the international prize for secularism for her book *Ma vie à contre-Coran* (*My life against the Qur'an*).

Averroès (p.47): Born in Cordoba, Andalusia, Averroès (1126-1198) was one of the greatest thinkers and philosophers of his time. He was also considered to be one of the founding fathers of secular thought. Towards the end of his life he was accused of apostasy and forced to leave Andalusia. He died in Marrakesh.

Khayam (p.47): Born in Iran, Khayam (1038 or 1048-1123 or 1124) was a philosopher, a mathematician, and a great poet known for his Rubayat. Following the publication of certain of his writings, he was accused of apostasy.

Abou Nawas (p.47): Born in Iran, Abou Nawas (762-813) spent most of his life in Iraq, where he died. Considered to be one of the greatest poets of the time of the Abbasids, he was nicknamed 'the poet of wine and love' and is known for his writings on the love of wine, of men, and on libertinage. He was also a staunch critic of religious institutions.

Ibn Arabi (p.47): Born in Andalusia, Ibn Arabi (1165-1240) died in Damascus. He was one of the greatest philosophers and Sufis of Andalusia, and was nicknamed 'the Master' or 'the perfect Man'.

Al-Mutanabbi (p.49): Al-Mutanabbi (915-965) is considered to be one of the greatest poets of all time. He was born in Iraq, but mostly lived in Aleppo, at the court of the Hamdanid emir Ali Sayfal-Dawla. His poems are, for the most part, hymns of praise for kings or descriptions of battles.

Al-Hallaj (p.49): Al-Hallaj (born in Iran in 857, died in Baghdad in 922) was a mystic poet and Sufi philosopher, and is considered to be one of the grand masters of Sufism. When he was sentenced to death, he is said to have shouted: 'Ana Al Haqq' ('I am the truth' or 'I am the supreme reality').

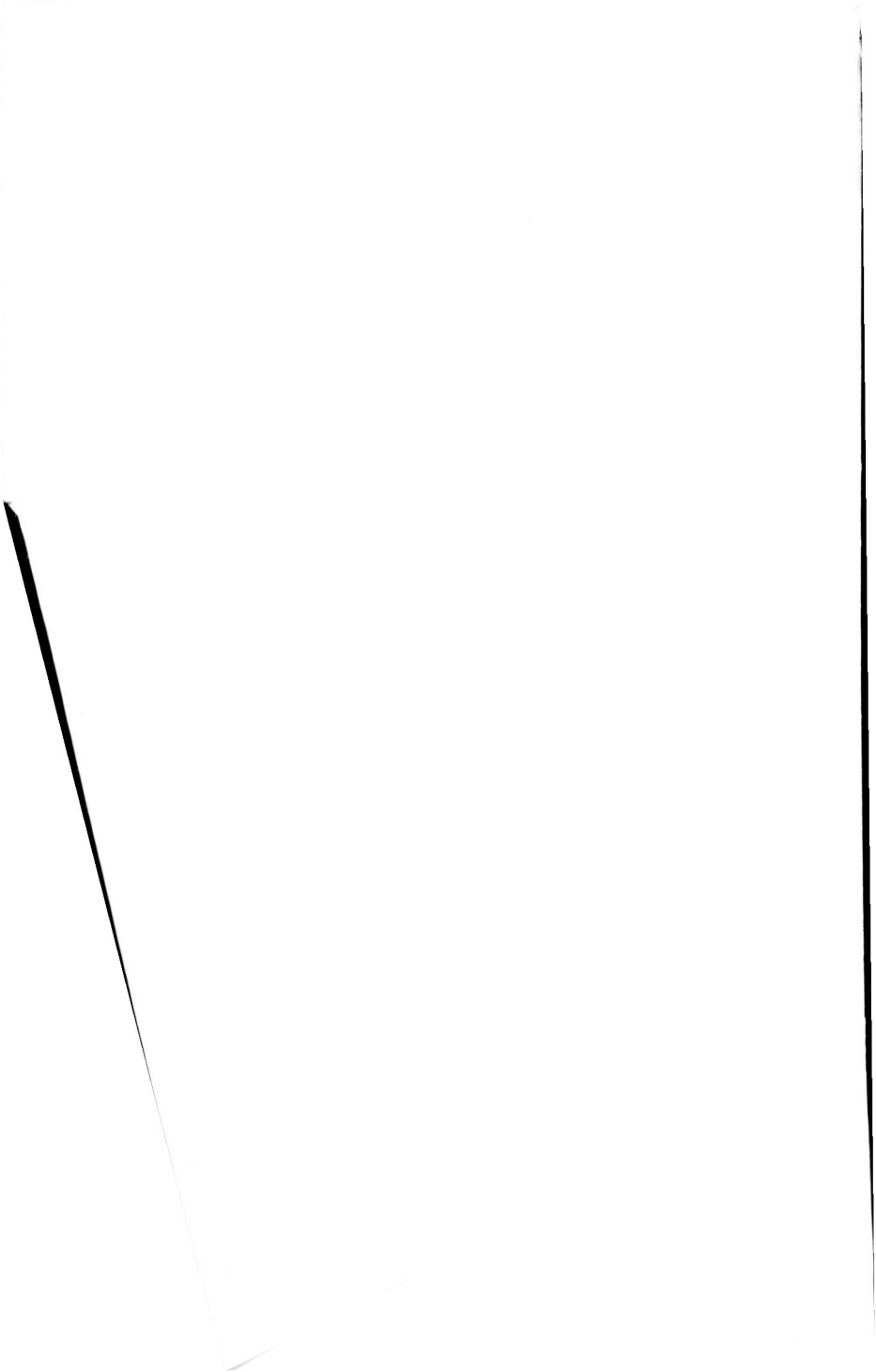

Naked Eye Publishing

A fresh approach

Naked Eye Publishing is an independent not-for-profit micro-press intent on publishing quality poetry and literature.

A particular focus is translation. We aim to take a midwife role in facilitating the translation of works that have until now been disregarded by English-language publishing. We will be happy if we function purely as an initial stepping-stone both for overlooked writers and first-time literary translators.

Each of us at Naked Eye is a volunteer, competent and professional in our work practice, and not intending to make a profit for the press. We see ourselves as part of the revolution in book publishing, embodying the newly levelled playing field, sidestepping the publishing establishment to produce beautiful books at an affordable price with writers gaining maximum benefit from sales.

nakedeyepublishing.co.uk

Milton Keynes UK
Ingram Content Group UK Ltd.
UKHW020728281124
3206UKWH00017B/149

9 781910 981184